No such place lasts summerlong

No such place lasts summerlong

Andrejs Eglitis
Velta Snikere

Poems

Introduction by Derek Stanford

International Poetry Society & HUB Publications Ltd
1974

Andrejs Eglitis' poems translated from the Latvian
by *Velta Snikere*.

Cover and typographic design
by *Normunds Hartmanis*.

Acknowledgement
Thanks are due to my daughter *Nora Ware* and to my friend *Robert Fearnley* for assistance in proof-reading and for helpful suggestions.
Velta Snikere

I.S.B.N. O 902707 84 1

HUB Publications Ltd.,
Youlgrave, Bakewell,
Derbyshire, England.
Printed in Sweden

Introduction

To Latvians of literary disposition, the two poets presented here — Andrejs Eglitis and Velta Snikere — need no introduction. They are known names, whether among their countrymen at home or in exile (some 400,000 of them having headed West after the Soviet annexation of their land at the end of the Second World War). English readers, however, may care for a word concerning these two authors who between them have published eighteen volumes and been translated into Italian, Spanish, German, Swedish, Norwegian, Danish, Estonian and Lithuanian.

It must have been over ten years ago that I first met Velta Snikere, an attractive and unassuming woman, in a course on modern poetry which I was holding at the City Literary Institute in London. Foreign students and distinguished birds of passage from Europe were then not infrequent visitors there — a leading Yugoslav writer drifting into my class about the same time. Paradoxically, language barriers sometimes heighten our curiosity, but Miss Snikere spoke an all-but-impeccable English, having been interpreter for the British Army in Austria in 1945 and settling in England the following year. Because of this, it took me some time — though I knew she wrote poetry herself — to learn of her place in the annals of contemporary Latvian verse. Probably the first mention of her name to the English reader occurred in the anthology A Century of Latvian Poetry, *translated and selected by Professor W. K. Matthews and published by John Calder in 1957. Along with her poem in that collection were three by her friend Andrejs Eglitis, a selection of whose poems she has made and translated from the Latvian in the present volume. Both poets have appeared widely in Latvian exile newspapers and journals and have read their work in Europe, the U.S.A. and Australia.*

Thus, when Miss Snikere approached me recently with the idea of bringing out a collection of her verse with that of Andrejs Eglitis in England, I was delighted to suggest she contact Robin Gregory with the hope that the International Poetry Society might be able to undertake publication. Mr. Gregory, I am glad to say proved as enthusiastic as myself.

The son of a musician killed in the First World War, Andrejs Eglitis was born in 1912. Editor of the Riga Radio Information Service, he fled by boat to Sweden in 1945 and is now a Swedish citizen. At a Conference of Baltic Studies held at the University of Toronto two years ago, Ivar Ivask pointed out that "the emotional involvement of Courland which fell to the Russians as late as May 1945, and the fact that organized armed resistance lasted in the Lithuanian forests until 1952, motivated Latvian and Lithuanian writers". The poems of Andrejs Eglitis are frequently the production of a strong patriotic imagination; and this is one of the elements which has been responsible for his wide reputation among his countrymen. In a volume of essays on Latvian Literature, Janis Andrups and Vitauts Kalve recall how a long poem written by Andrejs Eglitis was set to music by Lucija Garuta and heard for the first time in the Old Church of St. Gertrud, in Riga. The year was 1944, when the Latvian earth was indeed in flames. "When the German occupation forces devastated it and the Soviet invaders came bursting in from the East ... the church was overcrowded to its utmost capacity and the hearing of (the cantata) ... with its leading motif God, Thy Earth is Aflame ... was an experience never to be forgotten."

At the same time, the vivid and dynamic imagery in which he expresses these sentiments confers on them a validity beyond that of much patriotic feeling in verse:

>Distant motherland, what words will bridge for us?
>You bring tears and signs of war in dreams.
>Drunk with your tears, I rush at cliffs —
>It is like hitting against death, when I reach out for you.
>Armfuls of martyrs you are called to cradle.
>My distant motherland, to me, what are you?
>Heaven to rise into, burden to bow down under,
>Rites of purifying thunder before I may die.

A patriotic poetry is necessarily a social poetry; and in art which is turned towards — concerned with — society, we often notice an absence of individual emotion. In Andrejs Eglitis, however, the subjective and objective come powerfully together, as suggested by the following remark: "How do I regard my poetry? Like one looks into a mirror — my true self. Intention, to continue writing true poetry, especially on behalf of the millions oppressed and silenced in my motherland."

Before the impact of war, which made the poet "the most accomplished portrayer of the tragic experience of the Latvian nation," nature had been his foremost theme while stylistically he had come much under the influence of the French lyricists. Such pieces as Autumn, In the Fullness of Summer, *or the title-poem* No Such Place Lasts Summerlong *indicate these directions. Since the War, Andrejs Eglitis has sounded a note of protest — "Towering black gallows rise above you, Europe" — against the gathering landslide into life without principles in the name of principles that themselves spell death. Here, however, his work is represented by a small handful of patriotic poems together with a larger number which combine the simplicity of the folk song with the elegance of fashioned lyric.*

Miss Snikere's renditions of these poems are something other than a literal version. She has described her transposition into English as being "rather a recreation than a translation; there is divergence from the originals (with Andrejs' blessing) in words, expressions, images, rhythm," adding that "the spirit is the same."

Velta Snikere's father was a professor of medicine at Riga University where she herself studied philosophy. When she was thirteen, she commenced her Diary of the Mind, *a collection of aphorisms, having written poems since she was five. Shortly after coming to England, she became a member of the Chartered Society of Physiotherapy and, from time to time has worked in hospitals. She has always been a dancer and for some years was a member of Ram Gopal's Indian Dancers. Since 1966 she has been a teacher of Yoga at Greater London Council evening classes, and is a Yoga teachers' tutor.*

It has been said of Miss Snikere that she writes "subconsciously conceived poems bearing the stamp of surrealism." *Many of her poems seek to locate inner states in an outward language:*

> Here
> I stand
> On sand;
> The wind
> Scatters ashes
> Past my hand.
> Here I am blind
> Like the rest
> Of my kind.
> But there,
> Where I have been,
> I have seen.

Sometimes her lines sound like proverbs heard in a dream, maxims ennunciated in a folk-song: "Laugh yourself out/Of your skin of scars ... A peal of laughter./Peel off laughter."

The problem of the identity of things — their quiddity *or 'whatness' as Duns Scotus called it — is another issue her poems grapple with. Juris Kalns-Staune has spoken of her search "to find the words hidden in objects", and such a piece as* Things —

> What are the things
> That are things
> As they are

— reveals the same quest, though differently approached, which Rilke had in mind when he spoke, in one of his French poems of "the rose in itself; rose, only rose."

In conclusion, I cannot do better than quote what the eminent Latvian critics Janis Rudzitis and Vitauts Kalve, wrote of her work. "Her volume of poetry is slender, but it is one of the most exciting things that have happened in Latvian literature." My hope is that this excitement will spill over to stimulate the English reader.

Derek Stanford

Andrejs Eglitis

On guard over Couronia

Grass greener flourishes, and eagerly peer raven eyes, as
Over fermenting bog, marsh-rosemary tumbles on
Where, suddenly sinking, warriors' footprints end.
Up to the seashore woods gasp darkness, suffocating in decay.
A stinging dread drives stunned wolves to howl,
Where, in an unknown cemetery, Kursa's division holds.
Some bone or armour strikes the stranger's foot
And strikes at nations and the heart of days:
    Where is our land? Our land.
    Kurzeme!

But the red viper, strangling crawls Couronian fields.
On guard unchanging, long since mummified, a soldier stands,
To watch, his fallen head he holds, he holds in his hands.

You are the shore, one wishes to touch when drowning,
Reach with the tips of one's being.
When a lightning rich spring flashes across the sea
And I hear the first thunder from the direction of my motherland,
I know full well for whom I have saved loving words,
Whereto my every cell aspires, not to be restrained by any might.
To that ancient courtyard — renewed by bright lightning,
To those hollow sounding fjords, where grandmother told heavens
                              to stop scolding —
One can go in dreams and see expanses of black forests
Being ploughed by golden horses in undulating fiery bridles.
Passionately the first thunder resounds in the distances that have gone
                              grey with the passage of time.
And, as if young again, I straighten up and touch the skies
And I will hold them, keeping you safe for ever more.

Distant motherland, what words will bridge for us?
You bring tears and signs of war in dreams.
Drunk with your tears, I rush at cliffs —
It is like hitting against death, when I reach out for you.
Armfuls of martyrs you are called to cradle.
My distant motherland, to me, what are you?
Heaven to rise into, burden to bow down under,
Rites of purifying thunder before I may die.

Red-white-red

Weave me into red-white-red,
Weave me into our flag.
Then, as heaven weaves white morning flax
And the evening plaits its blood red tresses,
Let us gather flags, more flags, more flags than we are.
To be carried in the hands of all our dead,
Flags to flutter in the smiles of our unborn.
Weave me into our flag.
Our red-white-red,
Our sacred home.
It is there we dream.
In thinking of that, we wake.

Warrior laughter

Times worn dreadful
Bare their terror.
A bloodsplattered rider looms in the sky.
The vast burial ground screams with eagle-owls
And the river of the dead gargles and complains.
Everything threatens.
Mountains shudder and valleys lie low.
Attentively calm,
I hear my warrior laugh in battle,
In the storm on high of whirlwind hurricanes.
In the fielding of souls.
Calmly I sense my roots.
Mountains shudder, valleys lie low.
Fear not, my nation, your warrior laughs.

The swan

Freezing waters do not touch a swan.
Cold and ice, I beg of you, do not touch love!
Years, having grown old, stand round with icicle mouths.
Awakened by the warmth of dreams, bees swarm with the honey
							of dreams.
I beg of you, cold and ice, do not touch love.

The sun

At dawn the sun arises
And showers down its might.
I look through your disguises:
See only light.

Miraculous, yet silken,
The halo of your hair;
Far and wide there never was,
Never was one so fair.

By the sea we met
And meeting with the sea,
I promised to carry you
Over the sea —
Without sails or oars.
How could I, you asked:
— Our love has no shores —

Morning

The pale white doves of day alight
And soundlessly have lowered wings.
Your lowered lids
Keep out the light.

The pale white doves of day alight
With golden flames their trailing wings.
I share your overspilling light:
Gold bathes your breasts'
White birds.

The pale white doves of day alight
And silently have folded wings.
The sun, a captive in your heart.
You slumber.

Noon on the lake

Winds subside into sleep.
Fierce resplendence descends from the sky.
I shield my eyes, shield them in vain.

Winds stir and awaken the deep.
Steep brilliance outdazzles the sky.
To love you means to court pain.

Farewell

The vanishing wing of summer's last bird;
The evanescent scent of the last flower in the garden;
The sorrowful reflection of the disappearing rainbow:
I hear them.
I hear sad heavens crowding into your eyes for a funerary communion.
And I can hear the falling of weightless snow
As it falls and falls into the endless abysses of northern nights.
The sound of going away. My going.

Accept me

To slumber close to your arms,
Lightly, like falling snow;
Humbly then I would go
Into deep and eternal sleep.

Winds carry past as they journey.
The breath of winters since gone.
Winds and snow do not mourn me;
Accept me like light that has shone.

A river glistens
Through a flowering meadow,
The shadow of a bird
Hushes golden light.

Twilit tenderness
And the rushing of wings;
A trembling grass
Caresses my cheek.

I rise upon the humming wind,
Transparence, carry me:
To cast no shadow upon grass,
To cast no shadow.

With bated breath

With bated breath stands the forest.
Haltingly, out of hearing
Snowflakes alight upon branches
In this silent white clearing.

Homelesness. Shadows retaining
Footprints and roads disappear.
Snowflakes muffle all voices.
Only my heart can I hear.

Snowing skies and lost distance.
Snowflakes fall shadowless, boundless.
With bated breath stands the forest.
My heart, alone, speaks in the soundless.

The snow bunting

Snow-bunting comes running
To tell me winter is coming.
Hurrying envoy, within me
Winter arrived long ago.

Silent winter, protective,
Cover all that I see;
No spring will ever banish
The snow that has fallen in me.

Incomprehensible

Turn away and humbly close your eyes,
When a flame clad sun sets through the trees.
Kissing the earth, beauty passes by,
Incomprehensible.

Turn away and humbly close your eyes,
So as not to overburden grief:
Not all beauty
Can be yours to grasp.

Turn away and humbly close your eyes.
To God belongs the beauty of the birches,
When the evening guides red copper rivers
Round about the mighty hill of heaven.

Turn away and humbly close your eyes,
When a flame clad sun sets through the trees.
Kissing the earth, beauty passes by,
Incomprehensible.

Your gardens

Lord, your gardens miraculously flower!
My soul is blind.

Pebbles and planets proclaim your power!
My ear is deaf.

Like dew upon grass I am that clings
To the middle of the world, to the edge of things.

Beauty

A lamb, let out, frolicks and kneels
And openly its joy reveals.

A placid caterpillar feeds
Among the leaves on golden seeds.

In each damp blade a hot sun winks,
But who would dare to touch such drinks?

Back to the sheep the small lamb runs,
Around his feet set a hundred suns.

>   And when he met God, being such,
>   At once God liked him very much.

Grandmother holds up from the dew
Her splendid skirt of colours true.

And as behind the lamb she wades,
She far surpasses blooms and blades.

When dusk leaps up with darkening hue
She helps the lamb to find its ewe.

She gives him grass that's sweet and whole
Fresh from her sunlight flooded soul.

>   And when she met God, being such,
>   At once God liked her very much.

Grandfather's death

God's flowery kerchief
Joyfully flutters
When grandfather scatters
Crumbs for the dove.

Pecking at crumbs,
The dove, confidentially,
Urges grandfather
To walk beyond life.

A spider carefully
Crosses the window sill,
Grandfather calmly
Hears out the dove.

Briefly recalling
Starry night pastures:
What is it like
To be laid to rest?

A handful of seeds
And the tools of his youth
And the songs that he knew
He takes to eternity.

Leaving no footprints
Grandfather goes,
God's flowery kerchief
Spread on his path.

Open my eyes, summer, with the white lights of your purity, for the entering and deep penetration of your soul. Open my eyes for seeing beyond the slumber of the fully opened blossoms inside the dreams of the young fruit; for travelling beyond the fiery noon.
— May I see further than incomplete dreams of heaven, may I go further than the driven snow banished by spring, further and also nearer.

Autumn

How peacefully this day is introverting,
And fruit and honeycomb grow in transparence.
A shadow, only briefly disconcerting,
Darts past a slumbering, suspended moth.

Deeply rich colours interlace, reflect
No shivering leaf, no over-burdened fruit.
Slowly a spider spins into the light,
Casting mute golden threads across my face.

In the fullness of summer

Into garlanded days
Strikes sudden thunder,
Touching our apple tree,
Tears it asunder.

Fiercely the undergrowth fights,
The thorn and the fern.
Messenger, answer me —
Is it my turn?

White the petals fall.
Shall I halt beneath the tree
— White the petals fall —
Waiting to awake from life
By death's call?

At night

The light-eyed night, partaking of silence with me,
reads the ancient scripts leaning over my shoulder.
Acknowledge the truth of the eternal — to the end it
will be the same as of old — being born, dying, believing
or unbelieving — as of old.
The clairvoyant night perceives, my eyes and my soul
perceive the knotted riddles of the blue immortality
spiders.
Entering through the pages of the book, entering
through the riddled nets, I sense the gaiety of a
wild orchid's valley, face upturned, new born eternity.

Enough, says the night

Like a rose garden, washed in the blood of first creation,
flowering over, to heaven goes tonight — one has flowered
enough, enough, says the night.

The snow of dead, outdreamed hope vanishes also, fading
with drift upon drift of fragrant syringa.
Enough of dreaming, enough, says the night.

The lullaby of the cradle of love, the love impossible
to love to completion, calls my soul.
Enough, dear nurse, enough, says the night.

The nicked spear of dawn sharply recoils from my chest,
the shaft quivering as in battle — enough, true devoted,
enough, says the night.

Misty rivers and lakes, veiled diaphanously, like maidens
from beyond, offer the opalescent path of going and
coming. Enough, enough, night of my morning.

No such place lasts summerlong

Overhead the hissing firs
        and the humming birches
Discourse with the wandering winds,
        high above me blowing.

Like the winds I have no might
        to remain for ever:
No such place lasts summerlong,
        or can overwinter.

Ebb I must and I must flow,
        endlessly returning;
Smiling with the sleeping stones,
        flickering in fire.

Velta Snikere

Things

What are the things
That are things
As they are?

If one were to see them
As they were
Or will be?

Things opened like clams
Disclosing tenderness,
But my sympathy,
My approaching caress
As if by spells
Distilled them:

As if poured out of glass,
Without shells,
Through each other
Transparent, outlines.

Epitaph on a tea rose

Golden-veined life
In a wilting gilt cloak,
Languishing gold.

Dying veiled queen,
Slain by a knife.
A hand stung in vain
Leaves the blood
Of its life
In vain
Upon gold.

Reflective

Weeping.
Savouring
Eyes.

Cold tears on my throat.
Calm, folded hands
Leave them afloat.

Eyes of a brother

Your eyes, icily cold,
Most sombre brother,
Your eyes, fiery, bold,
Most daring brother,
Your eyes tenderly hold,
Gentlest of brothers,
Death.

Outlasting

Far into life with me
I took a rose.

None may speak;
Those that are left with a rose in their hair
May remember.

Far into life with me
I took a rose.
The rose that my hair had worn.

The dancer

Upon an evening, upon dusk descending,
You rose and turned, and turned and leapt
And we knew moment upon glorious moment
Join glittering infinity.

First you were like a mirror,
Reflecting a glint,
Then a shaft,
Then a flood of light.

You blazed.
But now,
The light that you were
Turns to darkness,
As through you,
Who have become transparence,
There steps into the night
Of our consciousness
Pure lustre.

And we too
Have become windows
For the whirling presence
As it sweeps
Round and round
As it sweeps
With tongues of fire
Round your ecstasy.

For a friend

You said we were two halves
Of one sea star
Before there was land.
And every time we meet,
Grief touches deep
Homesickness.

For anything

Do not put out your hand
For anything sticky or sweet,
Or meat;

Only for bone and land.
The bone of contention
And the land beyond hope.

Peoples' silence

Although unmentionable
At conference table,
The hushed-up story
Of an unfair tale
Will not go stale.

Crushed by the Russian bear
Eager for Baltic honey,
Plundered by the West —
Wilson has given away
Baltic money —
When does the fate of the Baltic States
Get a mention at UNO?

Where are the Baltic States?

In a peoples' coffin
On a mountain of peoples,
Chained by declarations
Of the right of human movement,
Snowed under, suffocated,
By declarations of the freedom to breathe,
Out of the way,
On Siberian labour camp ice,
The very face forgotten.

But ingrowing silence
Will condense and shatter
The iron cage
Of high-level conspiratory chatter
And break the stranglehold.

Truth will break out.

And I lost the way

All of what I had meant to bring,
I lost on the way.
No phare reached so far,
No flare soared my way
And there was no star.

Only the sea.
Only the scar
Of the loss of you
In me.

Duration

I have departed
Without walking away.
The pine trees tinkle with their clear glass needles.
Like whirling snow
Days warp around and round,
Oblivious of ending or beginning.

I have discovered
The most hidden path,
Close in on it,
A lid over an eye.
Like whirling snow
Days wrap around and round,
Oblivious of ending or beginning.

All these eyes,
With which you look at me
As though through windows,
I will face.

All these arms,
With which you repel me and embrace,
I renounce.

Quietly to enter alone,
Foot upon mark,
The dark thicket,
Only by touching
The bark
Of living trees,
Sensing the signs
To the secretive growing.

The brink

To be ready —
At this point
Means:
I cease.

I surrender
Gravity,
Ready
To fall.

Lingering
On the brink,
Grieving,
At the loss of me to myself,

I hopelessly listen
For a voice —
One voice
To call me back.

None.
Only you
Call across the gulf
Of everything I know.

But then — to your voice alone
I turn my ear;
Whoever else would call,
I would not hear.

Here
I stand
On sand.

The wind
Scatters ashes
Past my hand.

Here I am blind,
Like the rest
Of my kind.

But there,
Where I have been,
I have seen.

Here I walk and talk,
But there
I stand.

Light

Glittering sandals upon water,
Over water
Light wades into me;
Nothing protects my heart.

Depth protects the deep,
Lids protect the eye;
Nothing protects my heart.

To gain it, postpone understanding

Find your mind, make it up
To reach beyond reason;
Tread down desire
To stand above understanding.

And so as not to misunderstand,
Insist, yours is an empty hand
Until there is nothing
Out of grasp.

Lapis

Light poured out, to be attained within,
Innermost juice of pulsating;
Deeply silent
Until solidified:
Amber.

Identity

Skin after skin
To grow and make and break,
Grow a persona
And then drop the mask.

Unpeel the ego
Of its dawn and dusk.

Peel husk by husk, off,
Like a clever snake;

Or, like the onion,
Holding preciously,
Clasped sheath by sheath
The me that is not me,

But boundless space,
After its walls have gone,

Out of its pigeon-shelf,
Eternal self.

Swarming sunlight

I find myself
In unexpected places
And walk a beehive,
Multitudinous faces.

Golden drips honey down
From bees of swarming sunlight,
Healing bruises in stones
And scars in water.

Asked

It is mostly for mirrors,
That I have been asked.
As myriads of mirrors
I have stood,
Manifoldly masked.

It is mostly for mirrors,
That I have been asked.
As thousands of mirrors
I have stood,
A thousandfold masked.
And yet, to heal
I have been asked,
But not, to reveal.

When rulers were kings and Gods spoke without prophets —
— yet they tore Orpheus up.
Where now is the tongued diction?

As long as the secret serpent circles,
Spheres are disjointed
And no king anointed.

Those who can hear
The lament of the ancient bequest
Have to continue divining
The unguessed.

The secret serpent
In the sunken sea
And the hidden nest
In the golden plumed tree
Have to meet in me.

As yet you have again been so undone;
Who will collect you, Oziris, and make you one?

Life will groan,
As it wakes within stone,
Like a heart it will beat,
Knock in rock,
As it wakes within stone,
Will uncoil,
As it wakes in the soil.
Wakening Pharaoh.

You are bound

Space is round.
You are bound
To return.

When I call
You to fall,
Angel mine.

Like a hawk
On my hand
You must land,

Like an eagle
Its prey
Sweep me up.

Rorik

To be found.
To know
One is found.

Finding of the very sense of being found,
Unrivalled sense.

You called me and all there was,
Was your voice,
You called me from all directions at once

By a name I had never heard.
By a name I had not heard,
For an unending moment.
It was like mending
Of broken ends,
Like healing.
Like the awaited
Completion of the circle.

All that concerns me
Is complete
Within that voice,
Calling that name.

At the centre of me
An echo awoke,
How long since
Harboured within me?

All of me answered
In resonance,
All of me
Is your echo.

Your voice has found
Itself in me
From another time,
From another life;

It knows itself
My very roots,
The innermost thread
Of life.

Refrain

Not that I am strong,
But none is stronger,
Only your song.
Pray, how much longer
Will time be long
For the lack of your song?

Vanquish in love.
Let your turtle doves land on my shoulders and arms —
I will not startle them by turning sharply.
Let your flowers arise from my open palms —
Your butterflies will not alarm me,
Nor your nightingales . . .

Speak

Speak the words that have sealed your lips,
Forgetting sweet talk.
Speak the words that have stunned your tongue
And discard bitter talk.
Answer the words that have choked your throat,
That have broken your heart,
That have chilled your spine
And untwined your roots,
That have scared your guts
And laugh yourself out
Of your skin of scars.

Pause unassailable:
A peal of laughter.

Peel off laughter.

Andrejs Eglitis

Page
11 On guard over Couronia
12 *You are the shore*
13 *Distant motherland*
14 Red-white-red
15 Warrior laughter
16 The swan
17 The sun
18 *By the sea we met*
19 Morning
20 Noon on the lake
21 Farewell
22 Accept me
23 *A river glistens*
24 With bated breath
25 The snow bunting
26 Incomprehensible
27 Your gardens
28 Beauty
29 Grandfather's death
30 *Open my eyes, summer*
31 Autumn
32 In the fullness of summer
33 At night
34 Enough, says the night
35 No such place lasts summerlong

Velta Snikere

Page
39 Things
40 Epitaph on a tea rose
41 Reflective
42 Eyes of a brother
43 Outlasting
44 The dancer
45 For a friend
46 For anything
47 Peoples' silence
48 And I lost the way
49 Duration
50 *All these eyes*
51 The brink
52 *Here*
53 Light
54 To gain it, postpone understanding
55 Lapis
56 Identity
57 Swarming sunlight
58 Asked
59 *When rulers were kings and Gods spoke without prophets*
60 You are bound
61 Rorik
63 Refrain
64 *Vanquish in love*
65 Speak